George Herbert's 82

FRAMEWORKS

Interdisciplinary Studies for Faith and Learning

Previously published
volumes in the series:

What's So Liberal about the Liberal Arts?
Integrated Approaches to Christian Formation

Paul W. Lewis and
Martin William Mittelstadt, editors

Christian Morality: An Interdisciplinary Framework
for Thinking about Contemporary Moral Issues

Geoffrey W. Sutton and
Brandon Schmidly, editors

George Herbert's 82

Psalmic Social Disorientation
in
The Temple

Nathan H. Nelson

☙PICKWICK *Publications* · Eugene, Oregon

GEORGE HERBERT'S 82
Psalmic Social Disorientation in *The Temple*

Frameworks: Interdisciplinary Studies for Faith and Learning

Pickwick Publications
An Imprint of Wipf and Stock Publishers
199 W. 8th Ave., Suite 3
Eugene, OR 97401

www.wipfandstock.com

PAPERBACK ISBN: 978-1-5326-0610-6
HARDCOVER ISBN: 978-1-5326-0612-0
EBOOK ISBN: 978-1-5326-0611-3

Cataloguing-in-Publication data:

Names: Nelson, Nathan H., author
Title: George Herbert's 82 : psalmic social disorientation in *The Temple* / by Nathan H. Nelson.
Description: Eugene, OR: Pickwick Publications, 2019 | Series: Frameworks: Interdisciplinary Studies for Faith and Learning | Includes bibliographical references.
Identifiers: ISBN 978-1-5326-0610-6 (paperback) | ISBN 978-1-5326-0612-0 (hardcover) | 978-1-5326-0611-3 (ebook)
Subjects: LCSH: Herbert, George, 1593–1633. Temple. | Christian poetry, English—Early modern, 1500–1700—History and criticism.
Classification: PR3507.T43 N33 2019 (print) | PR3507.T43 (ebook)

Manufactured in the U.S.A.   APRIL 26, 2019

Series Preface

WE AFFIRM THE VALUE of a Christian liberal arts education. We believe that lifelong development of a Christian worldview makes us more fully human. We attest that engagement in the liberal arts contributes to the process of integrating Christian spirituality with a broad range of disciplinary studies. This integrative process requires that we explore and reflect upon biblical and theological studies while learning effective communication, pursuing healthy relationships, and engaging our diverse global community. We believe that the convergence of academic disciplines opens the door to the good life with enlarged promise for worship of the living God, development of deeper communities, and preparation for service and witness.

Our contributors are dedicated to the integration of faith, life, and learning. We celebrate exposure to God's truth at work in the world not only through preachers, missionaries, and theologians, but also through the likes of poets, artists, musicians, lawyers, physicians, and scientists. We seek to explore issues of faith, increase self-awareness, foster diversity, cultivate societal engagement, explore the natural world, and encourage holistic service and witness. We offer these studies not only as our personal act of worship, but as liturgies to prepare readers for worship and as an opportunity to wrestle with faith and practice through the arts and sciences.

In this series, we proclaim our commitment to interdisciplinary studies. Interdisciplinary studies involves the methodological combination of two or more academic disciplines into one research project.

Within a Christian worldview, we address complex questions of faith and life, promote cooperative learning, provide fresh opportunities to ask meaningful questions and address human need. Given our broad approach to interdisciplinary studies, we seek contributors from diverse Christian traditions and disciplines. Possibilities for publication include but are not limited to the following examples: 1) We seek single or multiple author contributions that address Christian faith and life via convergence of two or more academic disciplines; 2) We seek edited volumes that stretch across interdisciplinary lines. Such volumes may be directed specifically at the convergence of two or more disciplines and address a specific topic or serve as a wide-ranging collection of essays across multiple disciplines unified by a single theme; 3) We seek contributors across all Christian traditions and encourage conversations among scholars regarding questions within a specific tradition or across multiple traditions. In so doing we welcome both theoretical and applied perspectives.

The vision for this project emerged among professors at Evangel University (Springfield, MO). Evangel University, owned and operated by the General Council of the Assemblies of God (AG), is the fellowship's national university of arts, sciences, and professions: the first college in the Pentecostal tradition founded as a liberal arts college (1955). Evangel University is a member institution of the Council for Christian Colleges and Universities (CCCU). Consistent with the values and mission of the AG and CCCU, Evangel University exists to educate and equip Christians from any tradition for life and service with particular attention to Pentecostal and Charismatic traditions. Evangel University employs a general education curriculum that includes required interdisciplinary courses for all students. The Evangel University representatives for this series continue to participate in the articulation and development of the Evangel University *ethos* and seek contributors that demonstrate and model confessional integration not only for the Evangel University community and Pentecostals, but all Christians committed to the integration of faith, learning, and life. We offer this series not only as a gift from the Evangel University community to other Christian communities interested in the intersection of intellectual integration and spiritual and societal transformation, but also as an invitation to walk with us on this journey. Finally, in order to ensure a broad conversation, our editorial committee includes a diverse collection of scholars not only from Evangel University but also from other traditions, disciplines, and academic institutions who share our vision.

SERIES EDITORS

EDITORIAL BOARD

For Thomas Clayton and George T. Wright,
esteemed teachers
much emulated, too little thanked

Contents

Chapter 1

Herbert's Ratios of Psalmic Intertextuality in *The Temple*[1]

GEORGE HERBERT'S LITERARY-CRITICAL STATURE as a poet in our day has not been established primarily by his echoes and emulations of the Hebrew Psalms, but they have certainly contributed to a consensus that the Old Scriptures were near his mind's eye and ear.[2] The resonances range from overt paraphrases to the merest suggestion raised by intense figuration. In *The Temple*, for instance, "The 23rd Psalm" begins with the obvious shadow-lines "The God of love my shepherd is, / And he that doth me feed"; but "Grief," which does not emulate an entire psalm, does deal in Old Scripture-style hyperbole about the physical effects of emotional torment: "Let ev'ry vein / Suck up a river to supply mine eyes, / My weary weeping eyes[. . .]." The lines are clearly in the same registers of sorrow and verbal extravagance as Ps 6:6, "Every night I make my bed swim, / I dissolve my couch with my tears" (NASB), and Jer 9:1, "Oh that my head were waters / And my eyes a fountain of tears, / That I might weep day and night / For the slain of the daughter of my people!" (NASB).

1. An earlier version of this essay appeared in a festschrift for longtime Evangel University professors Jim and Twila Edwards (Lewis and Mittelstadt, *What's So Liberal about the Liberal Arts?*, 141–53).

2. In his introduction to *Music for a King*, Coburn Freer remarks that "[a] poet and parson like Herbert, who recommended metrical psalms to his parish, who sang metrical songs, and could write perhaps the best single psalm of his age, invites a reading within the context of psalmody" (2).

Much attention has been given to Herbert's biblical intertextuality, and in Helen Wilcox's recent (2007) edition of Herbert's poems, she finds so many psalmic borrowings and emulations that they warrant a thick index of resonant psalms split out from her larger Index of Biblical References.[3] C. A. Patrides remarks that "almost every aspect of Herbert's poetry is traceable to the Bible," particularly to the "palpable influence of wisdom literature, of the Psalter, and of the parables embedded in the Gospels."[4]

On the other hand, *The Temple* cannot be seen as a competitor for the laurels in the period's vogue of psalm-emulations, metrical or otherwise. Beth Quitslund has shown that the mixed reception of the literarily adventurous Sidney Psalter of 1599 (more suitable for "chamber" devotional use than for congregational singing in church) provided a cautionary example for later poets such as Milton and Herbert, both of whom for the most part eschewed writing metrical psalm paraphrases suitable for corporate singing.[5] Milton, she claims, came to use classical epic and tragedy as the "vehicle[s] of divine poetry," and Herbert "chose to write the 'original' lyric corpus of 'The Church' instead of a metrical psalter."[6] Quitslund sees *The Temple* as a literary—but not fully psalmic—descendant of the Sidney psalter; it is great "devotional verse" better seen as a major step in the development of the English lyric. Just as the heightened poetic sophistication of the Sidney Psalms reduced their usefulness for public, corporate worship,[7] Herbert's daring flights of what we now call

3. Herbert, *The English Poems*, 727. Wilcox uses the Authorized Version (KJV) for all biblical references except those to the Psalms, for which she uses the Book of Common Prayer translation that would have been in Herbert's hands. In this essay, I generally use the Authorized Version for its resonances with Herbert's language and time as well as for easy articulation with Wilcox's findings.

4. Patrides, *Figures in a Renaissance Context*, 120.

5. The reception was limited, of course, by the fact that the Sidney Psalms, a gift in manuscript to Queen Elizabeth in 1599, were circulated only in hand-copied manuscripts, sixteen of which are known to have been made between 1590 and 1630 (see Brennan, "Licensing the Sidney Psalms," 304). The complete collection was not published as a book until 1823 (the Chiswick Press edition). Psalms 1–43 were composed by Sir Philip and Psalms 44–150 after his death by his sister, Mary Sidney Herbert, Countess of Pembroke.

6. Quitslund, "Teaching Us How to Sing?," 109–10.

7. See Quitslund, "Teaching Us How to Sing?," 103–4. Quitslund takes

"metaphysical" fancy seem to disqualify most of the poems included in *The Temple* for the same purpose. Quitslund's point is well taken, but in this discussion I want to use the word *psalter* in the qualified sense of "a book of songs written in the *spirit* of the Hebrew psalter with some emulation of its varying moods and topics on something like the same scale."[8] The usage is not entirely figurative. Such a book would admittedly be far enough from the liturgical ideal of careful translation or paraphrase to make the term *psalter* seem metaphoric to Hebrew scholars—but I am interested in Herbert's refractions of biblical psalmody for his own sensitive soul and, by Nicholas Ferrar's fortunate preservation, for that of any reader.

Wilcox, citing work by John N. Wall, notes that "the parallels between Herbert's poems and the psalms even include the numerical, in that the number of poems in *The Church* [sic; the longest section of *The Temple*] is the same as that of the psalms as divided up for liturgical use in the Church of England calendar."[9] Furthermore, we can see that, having 163 poems, "The Church" is of the same order of magnitude as the number of poems in the canonic Book of Psalms: 150. These signs of Herbert's possibly motivated imitation should make us wonder how deeply his conscious or unconscious emulation ran. Wilcox's careful tracking and indexing of psalmic allusions in *The Temple* encourage further scrutiny of the poems' intertextuality. If "The Church" is his psalter, we might look beyond lexical similarity into the complexities of collection-structure, thematic poem-grouping, rhetorical-liturgical modalities, and postures of supplication. Much scholarship has recognized *The Temple*'s high ratio of concern about personal spiritual rectitude, and it is commonly understood that the Psalms themselves have a high ratio of

---

considerable pains to show that the Sidney Psalter is difficult to sing, and she seems to suggest that its language is at times a bit too difficult for a common congregant to understand readily.

8. Wilcox admits that "Herbert's biblical inspiration is often what we might call subterranean" (*The English Poems of George Herbert*, xvii), but the occasional direct allusion and the narrative or topical structure keep suggesting at least passing intertextuality with the Psalms.

9. Wilcox, *The English Poems of George Herbert*, xxviii. Wilcox cites Wall's *Transformations of the Word*, 170. Note: Wilcox uses italics for all titles; I will use them for the title of the entire collection, *The Temple*, but I will use quotation marks for the sub-collection called "The Church."

individual concern—that is, concern for the well-being of the psalms' personae, spiritual or otherwise.[10] Somewhat less attention has been given to Herbert's concern over personal and corporate *social* rectitude exclusive of his own court experiences and hopes. This paper will investigate the degree to which Herbert addresses matters of social concern like those found in the Book of Psalms.

Biblical scholars have long attempted to categorize the Hebrew psalms in order to understand their topical and generic contributions to cultic worship in ancient Israel. Many systems ranging from the simple to the complex have been suggested, but the overlaps from system to system are significant enough to allow some reasonable hybridization to be done. Following the work of Hermann Gunkel and Claus Westermann, W. H. Bellinger Jr. suggests the following classification of the Hebrew psalms:[11]

- Praise Psalms
- Lament Psalms
- Royal Psalms
- Wisdom Psalms

Bellinger subdivides the "Praise" category into eight subclasses and the "Lament" category into two. For each category and subclass, he supplies a list of psalms that seem to fit. Our interest in Herbert's "psalter" can lead us to consider whether or not "The Church" has anything like the category ratios that Bellinger sees in the biblical collection.

According to Bellinger's analysis, sixty-one of the Hebrew psalms (40.67 percent) are of the "Praise" variety; sixty-seven (44.66 percent) are "Lament" poems; eleven (7.33 percent) are "Royal"

---

10. Old Testament scholar Hermann Gunkel in *The Psalms* resists an ancient tendency to allegorize the psalmic speaking voices (the *personae*) that refer to themselves as "I." In many psalms, he says, "an allegorical interpretation of the 'I' would result in a very unnatural understanding of the psalm. Thus we maintain that, apart from a few isolated cases, the 'I' almost invariably refers to the individual, and that therefore we have in the Psalms a rich collection of poetry of the individual" (16–17).

11. Bellinger, *Psalms*, 23. See Gunkel, *Introduction to Psalms* and *The Psalms: Form-Critical Introduction*.

psalms; and eleven (7.33 percent) are "Wisdom" psalms.[12] Although Bellinger's classification of individual psalms undoubtedly has some idiosyncratic bias, it is nevertheless striking to find that the largest category of Hebrew psalms appears to be that of lament.[13] Claus Westermann argues, in fact, that the lament is the *ur*-form underlying virtually all of the Hebrew psalms and their variety of secondary forms,[14] and Walter Brueggemann has observed "a close correspondence between *the anatomy of the lament psalm* [. . .] and *the anatomy of the soul.*"[15] This latter phrase clearly describes a great number of Herbert's poems in "The Church."

Much like Brueggemann, Norman Gottwald understands the lament psalms to be commentaries on issues of social concern and justice.[16] In other words, both scholars would encourage us not to spiritualize the psalms (or to select only the most spiritually "uplifting") to the point at which the concrete, historical differentials of power and privilege in the ancient Hebrew world become invisible. Given that Herbert's collection called "The Church" may be considered his psalter, we may reasonably ask how much of the collection participates in the biblical mode of lamentation for a disoriented society. Here we must often distinguish poems of individual lament from poems of corporate lament.

Many of Herbert's poems begin in some condition of lamentable unrest; some end in rejoicing or at least satisfaction. They pose most of the same difficulties of classification that scholars have had

---

12. All numbers in the sentence are mine. Bellinger simply lists the psalms in each category by their canonic numbers.

13. Other scholars may differ about the numbers of psalms in each category, and they may "cross-list" some psalms in more than one category. Gunkel, for example, considers the Asaphic Psalm 82 an "Eschatological Hymn" (*The Psalms*, 31), a courtroom drama with prophetic judgment speech (*Introduction*, 279–80), and a liturgy-with-oracle (*Introduction*, 284 and 317). He is much interested in the antiphonal qualities of the psalm, to which he provides background in *Introduction*, 310–17.

14. Reported by Brueggemann in *Message of the Psalms*, 18. See Westermann's *Praise and Lament*, Part One, "The Categories of the Psalms," esp. 31 and 34.

15. Brueggemann, *Message of the Psalms*, 18–19.

16. In Bellinger's "Excursus: The Psalms and Sociology" (*Psalms* 146–50), he summarizes Gottwald's arguments at length, referring to *The Hebrew Bible*, 522–41.

with the Psalms, but it is not very difficult to see that most of the poems in "The Church" are about individual (rather than corporate or social) struggles, needs, complaints, or praises.

In dealing with the biblical psalms of lament (sixty-seven by his analysis), Bellinger further distinguishes "Individual Psalms" from "Community Psalms," supplying the following ratio: fifty "Individual" and seventeen "Community" psalms. Thus, 33.33 percent of the Psalter is of the "Individual Lament" sort, and 11.33 percent is of the "Community Lament" sort. Of these groupings, the more obvious match with Herbert's poetry is the first. Most of Herbert's personae can, with reason, be described as proto-monastic, or (with a somewhat different timbre) at least puritan, for they fall easily into meditative melancholy lending itself to personal lamentation, which includes the whole range of topics about human discomfort and distress. Because both High Church and Low/Dissident Church traditions endorse versions of spiritual self-analysis, scholars have mightily exercised themselves in trying to determine where Herbert stood on the spectrum from Calvinism to Arminianism, but in his published work Herbert still seems to elude them all by exhibiting a practical ecumenism based in Scripture. As Christopher Hodgkins has observed, "[Herbert's] spirit was typical of neither" the more-Calvinist Jacobean church nor the more-Arminian Caroline church (under Laud):

> James [I] led a church that was tolerant by default, while the Arminians made one that was unyieldingly and swiftly coercive. Neither had much use for conscience. In contrast, Herbert was a man of great inner spaces whose spiritual experience produced a mind at once highly principled, humbly practical, and deeply respectful of that region called the heart, near the conscience, where no one but God has the prerogative or the power to move.[17]

In short, it is not hard to find Herbert's modal, if not directly allusive, emulations of the "Individual Lament" psalms, particularly those dealing with some perceived alienation from God or God's righteousness.

17. Hodgkins, *Authority, Church, and Society*, 85.

On the other hand, we know that Herbert understood and acted upon scriptures that, from a Christian perspective, are centered in the profundity of the Second Great Commandment: "Love thy neighbor as thyself."[18] His injunctions and examples in the long *Temple* poem "The Church-porch" and in the manual-like prose didacticism of *The Countrey Parson* are lengthy cases in point. In fact, the poet-priest's reputation as "Holy Mr. Herbert" has grown to such legendary status that it has recently been attacked as a debilitating influence upon today's Church of England ministers, who simply cannot do all that Herbert's reputation or his *Countrey Parson* require.[19] Judging by the social-concern standards set in "The Church-porch" and *The Countrey Parson*, and cognizant of Herbert's penchant for psalm-emulation throughout *The Temple*, we might expect to find a significant number of poems having social-concern topicality in the section called "The Church." By reference to Bellinger's accounting of the biblical model, we might use 11.3 percent as an informal criterion.

By collating Wilcox's index of Psalm-references in *The Temple* with Bellinger's psalm-categories, I have generated a provisional table showing the relative frequencies and percentages of Herbert's Psalm-emulation per category—as far as Wilcox's analysis extends:

18. Of course, this NT scriptural injunction (Matt 22:39, Mark 12:31, Luke 10:27, Rom 13:8, Gal 5:14, Jas 2:8, I John 3:17, I John 4:7) has its roots in many OT passages (Lev 19:18, Isa 58, Amos 5, and Mic 6:8 resonantly among them).

19. Lewis-Anthony, *If You Meet George Herbert*, 215; see also 5–22. At the time of this provocatively titled book's publication (2009), Lewis-Anthony was Rector of St. Stephen's Church in Canterbury.

Herbert's Psalm References Per Bellinger Type[20]			
Bellinger's Classification of the Psalms	Herbert's References Per Type	Herbert's Percentage of Total References Per Type	Bellinger's Percentage of the Book of Psalms Per Type
I. Praise	98	40.00	40.66
General Hymn	30	12.24	12.67
Creation	15	6.12	3.33
Enthronement	8	3.27	4.67
Zion	4	1.63	4.00
Entrance	4	1.63	1.33
Hymn w/Prophetic Warnings	0	0.00	2.00
Trust	14	5.71	3.33
Individual Thanks	19	7.76	5.33
Community Thanks	4	1.63	4.00
II. Lament	101	41.23	44.66
Individual Lament	84	34.29	33.33
Community Lament	17	6.94	11.33
III. Royal Psalms	19	7.76	7.33
IV. Wisdom Psalms	27	11.02	7.33

The results (to be discussed shortly) should probably not be surprising, since Herbert's own devotional life as well as his pastoral life was saturated with the full range of Hebrew psalm-topicality prescribed for twice-daily reading by the 1559 *Book of Common Prayer*: "AT THE MORNING AND EVENING PRAYER THROUGHOUT THE

---

20. This table represents my collation of Wilcox's "Index of Biblical References, Part 2: Psalms" with Bellinger's "Classification of the Psalms." All calculations and figures are mine.

YERE, [. . .] THE Psalter shalbe readde through, ones euery moneth [. . .]."[21]

My analysis of Wilcox's Index allows me to make the following observations: by her interpretation and accounting as well as her reporting of other scholars' findings, Herbert recognizably refers in some fashion to at least ninety-five of the 150 Psalms. Wilcox does not find and does not report others' finding *Temple* references to fifty-five of the Psalms (36.67 percent). Obviously, Wilcox's net may not have caught every allusion or parallel, but her careful work over all 163 poems in *The Temple* provides a heavily significant sample of likely references. Notice, in the table, the striking similarity of percentages between (a) the biblical distribution of psalms in categories according to Bellinger's analysis and (b) Herbert's references to psalms in those categories. "Praise" poems in the Psalter are 40.66 percent of the total; Herbert's references to "Praise" psalms constitute 40 percent of his total allusiveness to the Psalms as recorded by Wilcox. Bellinger finds 44.66 percent of the Psalter composed of "Lament" poems; Herbert's references to "Lament" psalms make up 41.23 percent of his recognized psalmic allusiveness. "Royal" psalms constitute 7.3 percent of the Psalter; Herbert's references to "Royal" psalms compose 7.76 percent of his total references. The biblical "Wisdom" psalms compose 7.33 percent of the Psalter; Herbert's "Wisdom"-psalm references constitute 11.02 percent of his recognized psalmic references. These are remarkably similar figures that tempt one to suspect Herbert of matching by plan. It is probably not possible to determine whether or not Herbert had any intention of matching the volume or weight-distribution of topics or types in the Psalms, but perhaps his careful attention to the biblical texts by devotional rule simply gave him a more and more thorough "feel" for the particular balance of the Hebrew collection.

By my accounting of Wilcox's editorial scholarship, at least ninety-five of the 163 poems in "The Church" are demonstrably intertextual with biblical psalms.[22] My own analysis suggests that twenty-five make some reference to issues of social concern (a category that overlaps heavily with that of Community Lament), but most of the

---

21. Wohlers, *Book of Common Prayer*.

22. In Norman Fairclough's terms, many of the intertextualities are *manifest*; others are *constitutive*. See *Discourse and Social Change*, 117.

poems are not wholly or even largely about such issues.[23]   While approximately 15.34 percent of the poems in "The Church" broach social-concern topics to any extent at all, only seven—"Content," "Humilitie," "Constancie," "Charms and Knots," "Church-rents and schismes," "Avarice," and "The Answer"—seem to qualify as strong treatments of social concern as Bellinger defines them. Another seven poems provide fairly substantial treatments of social concern issues (see Appendix). All together, the poems prominently featuring social concern in "The Church" number only around ten to fourteen by my analysis, so the ratio of social-concern poems in the collection is approximately 6.13–8.58 percent. The biblical psalms of "Community Lament" are not all about social justice or probity, but those topics do fit the category. Herbert's "community" psalms are few, and they are almost exclusively about those topics. Comparing his figures to Bellinger's listing and percentage of "Community Lament" psalms in the Psalter (11.33 percent), I find that Herbert appears to have produced only half to three-quarters (54–75 percent) as many "Community Lament" (or social-concern) poems as the number that appear in the Psalter. We can only speculate about reasons. Perhaps Herbert would have written more such poems if he had lived longer and seen more of the coming political storm. Perhaps he spent more time in the "Individual Lament" mode because of his own personal inclination toward monastic melancholy. Perhaps he consciously or unconsciously stayed on the fence between high-church and low-church spirituality by writing about personal holiness within a poetic tradition with immense and ancient liturgical credibility. This last speculation would, of course, add fuel to the fire of controversy over Herbert's "truest" ecclesial allegiance.

23. See the Appendix. My working criterion for a poem's inclusion is extremely low—on the order of lines 13–14 in "The H. Scriptures I," which say of the Bible, "Thou art joys handsell: heav'n lies flat in thee, / Subject to ev'ry mounters bended knee"; or lines 9–10 in "Repentance," which say, "we are all / To sorrows old." Both are extremely brief nods to egalitarian verities; neither conceit is developed further in the poem. In "Trinitie Sunday," the penitential *telos* of the poem clearly makes its social-concern aspects subdominant: "And sanctifi'd me to do good" is a moment's reference to good works during the earnest prayer for purgation of sins, and "Enrich my heart, mouth, hands [...] / With [...] charitie" is another, slightly less direct.

In making my analysis, I have considered a passage of Herbert's poetry to have a social-concern factor if it simply refers literally or figuratively for even the briefest period to any sort of interaction, obligation, or comparison between human beings on earth. The range of social-concern topics can run from broken or lamentably unestablished relationship (what Brueggemann would call *disorientation*) to whole, proper, and salutary companionship (*orientation, re-orientation, new orientation*[24]), the latter usually based upon some sense of mutual understanding or obligation. The range of rhetorical treatments of the topics can run from (a) mere naming or description of a problem through (b) didactic prescription for, and exemplification of, its solution to (c) description of a blessed state or condition of human relationship. Obviously, poems of the last sort may not qualify as *laments*, so they would be part of the "social concern" category that does not overlap with that of Community Laments or Individual Laments. Psalm 133, for example, is clearly a song about healthy (well-"oriented") human relationship:

> 1 Behold, how good and how pleasant it is for brethren to dwell together in unity!
>
> 2 It is like the precious ointment upon the head, that ran down upon the beard, even Aaron's beard: that went down to the skirts of his garments;
>
> 3 As the dew of Hermon, and as the dew that descended upon the mountains of Zion: for there the Lord commanded the blessing, even life for evermore. (KJV)

A Song of Ascent that Bellinger classifies among the "Wisdom Psalms," Psalm 133 extravagantly uses two concatenated similes and the expressed tenor of the overarching figure to recommend a condition of social bliss made possible by willing human agents. Herbert's poem most similarly indulgent in the good feelings of proper social *orientation* may be "Constancie," in which the character of "the honest man" is held up in seven stanzas as the "Mark-man" whose "goodnesse sets not" when the sun sets.

The further a poem may be situated toward the "disorientation" end of the social-concern spectrum, the more likely it is to be a lament or to refer to lamentable social (interpersonal) conditions.

24. See Brueggemann's own definitions of his terms in *Message*, 19–21.

Thus, God, represented as speaking in Ps 50:19–21, descends to specifics of social injustice and issues a prophecy:

> 19 Thou givest thy mouth to evil, and thy tongue frameth deceit.
>
> 20 Thou sittest and speakest against thy brother; thou slanderest thine own mother's son.
>
> 21 These things hast thou done, and I kept silence; thou thoughtest that I was altogether such an one as thyself: but I will reprove thee, and set them in order before thine eyes. (KJV)

Such disorientation can only be humanly redressed by "him that ordereth his conversation aright" (v. 23b)—the one who lives among others with proper respect for them and with proper demonstration of compassion and good will. It is no wonder that Bellinger places Psalm 50 into the same small subcategory with Psalm 82—"Hymns with Prophetic Warnings"—for both have an "angry God" speaker and a prophetic pronouncement for the socially malfeasant.

No poem in Herbert's "The Church" quite strikes that pair of notes, but "Unkindnesse" presents one of the longest of Herbert's reflections upon social probity. Ironically, however, the poem is not primarily about "horizontal" relationships or social justice. Its persona refers to his appropriate social behavior in four situations in order to contrast his treatment of *Christ* as shockingly disoriented in a manner that would be unthinkable to the persona in regard to his merely human friends. The judgment quality of the poem comes in the final lines, where the persona admits to treating Christ ("My God upon a tree") as worse than a foe. The unspoken suggestion is that the persona has thus apparently jeopardized his hope of salvation. Wilcox renders the poem as follows:

Unkindnesse.

Lord, make me coy and tender to offend:
In friendship, first I think, if that agree,
Which I intend,
Unto my friends intent and end.
I would not use a friend, as I use Thee.

If any touch my friend, or his good name;
It is my honour and my love to free
His blasted fame
From the least spot or thought of blame.
I could not use a friend, as I use Thee.

My friend may spit upon my curious floore:
Would he have gold? I lend it instantly;
But let the poore,
And thou within them starve at doore.
I cannot use a friend, as I use Thee.

When that my friend pretendeth to a place,
I quit my interest, and leave it free:
But when thy grace
Sues for my heart, I thee displace,
Nor would I use a friend, as I use Thee.

Yet can a friend what thou hast done fulfill?
O write in brasse, *My God upon a tree*
His bloud did spill
Onely to purchase my good-will:
Yet use I not my foes, as I use Thee.

Although "Unkindnesse" is primarily an individual lament about relationship with God (i.e., a spiritual relationship), the examples of proper social behavior function as an extended simile of how Christ should be treated—but it is negated five times in order to figure the extent of the spiritual sin. In other words, the tenor of the figuration has to do with the spiritual problem; the references to proper and improper social behavior (or justice) are just the vehicle of the figure. In stanza 3, lines 13–14, the two types of sin are conflated in the sense of Matthew 25:31–46, wherein Jesus explains the malfeasance of the "goats" as opposed to the behaviors of the "sheep." In "Unkindnesse," the deadliest wrong is that of failing to recognize and help the suffering Christ by "let[ting] the poore, / And *thou within* them starve at door" (my italics to emphasize the reference to Christ as "one of the least of these"). By ending the poem on the note of his treating the dying Christ worse than a foe, Herbert's persona leaves us without explicit solution to the problem. The implicit solution is to act justly in every aspect of one's life, spiritually as well as socially. In this regard, Herbert mingles the two concerns, again making it difficult to pin him down as a Calvinist or an Arminian; however, it is difficult to call "Unkindnesse" truly a social-concern poem unless we say it is so "by indirection."

On the other hand, I do not mean to disparage the value of any indirect, sidelong, or tangential social-concern gesture in Herbert's work. The mixed case of "Unkindnesse" does alert us to ask whether or not the notes of communal lament or social concern are sounded in poems of generally other sort in *The Temple.* If we consider the many highly introspective poems to be expressions of a Puritan, or at least Reformed, concentration upon personal holiness, it is but a short step to recognize that such holiness was thought to be the molecular transformative element in society. In Puritan reasoning, social righteousness could theoretically come about by multiplying the number of righteous individuals and their salutary effects upon society. Thus a reader of even Herbert's most individualistic poems might legitimately stay alert for the irruption of some social concern triggered by a process or moment of introspection. That other discourse may not be long or loud, but if it is there, Herbert should certainly be given credit for allowing its voice to be heard.

Christopher Hodgkins remarks that "moments of explicit social awareness are rare in 'The Church,'" but he suggests that, all together, its poems could have a "Tudor humanist" effect upon readers whose "transformed spiritual and intellectual li[ves]" may "overflow naturally in good works."[25] Tudor humanism is hardly the spirit that the Puritan reformers would have found sufficient in Christians of their day, so perhaps it was politic for Herbert to keep the casually perceived social-justice/personal-holiness ratio of his poetic output to a figure no greater than that of the Psalms themselves. In the

---

25. Hodgkins, *Authority, Church, and Society,* 206–7.

following section, however, I intend to demonstrate that Herbert's expressed understanding of and poetic engagement with biblical social justice goes somewhat further and deeper than the assumptions of Herbert scholarship to date. Of the twenty-five poems from *The Temple* that I have identified in the Appendix as showing at least marginal social concern, four are interestingly among the sixteen works by Herbert that Robert H. Ray has found most "popular" for allusion among seventeenth-century British writers: "Affliction (I)," "Charms and Knots," "Content," and "Man." In Ray's study, they are ranked numbers 4, 5, 7, and 11, respectively.[26] By that measure, 25 percent of the most contemporaneously and commonly alluded-to poems in Herbert's corpus call some degree of attention to matters of proper relationship between human beings. Two of those poems, "Content" and "Charms and Knots," have substantial, dedicated social-concern aspects that can hardly have been missed or misinterpreted by readers of the Commonwealth and Restoration periods. In "Content," a problem-of-vocation poem that Wilcox calls "unusually introverted,"[27] Herbert uses egalitarian notions to recommend self-discovery rather than social advancement by profession, repeatedly leveling the ground upon which kings and "private bodies" stand (ll. 13–16 and 21–24):

> Give me the pliant minde, whose gentle measure
>   Complies and suits with all estates;
> Which can let loose to a crown, and yet with pleasure
>   Take up within a cloisters gates.
>
> . . . .
>
> The brags of life are but a nine dayes wonder;
>   And after death the fumes that spring
> From private bodies, make as big a thunder,
>   As those which rise from a huge King.

26. Ray, "Herbert's Seventeenth-Century Reputation," 4. If we consider only the poems from "The Church" on Ray's list, those four would be ranked #2, 3, 5, and 9, respectively.

27. Wilcox, *The English Poems*, 250.

> Onely thy Chronicle is lost; and yet
>> Better by worms be all once spent,
> Then to have hellish moths still gnaw and fret
>> Thy name in books, which may not rent [. . .].

Here respect for the human individual regardless of social status or profession is loudly evident.

Even though some scholars of our time find the strikingly blunt "Charms and Knots" unworthy of inclusion in *The Temple*,[28] its "deliberately strained homeliness"[29] probably accounts for much of the poem's apparent popularity in the seventeenth century. If "The Church," as I have suggested, is Herbert's psalter, then a clunky poem in octosyllabic couplets more emulative of the Book of Proverbs does seem a bit out of place; nevertheless, its high rank (number 5) in Ray's accounting of Herbert allusions suggests that British writers of the time assumed wide readerly recognition of the poem, perhaps because, as Ray notes, "readers were evidently attracted to the pleasurable [couplet] form of his Christian didacticism."[30] If wide recognition bespoke approval as well, it is clear that homiletic values rooted in the Second Great Commandment and egalitarian sentiment must have been widely seen and appreciated in the poem, especially in lines 3–6 and 9–14:

> A poore mans rod, when thou dost ride,
> Is both a weapon and a guide.

> Who shuts his hand, hath lost his gold:
> Who opens it, hath it twice told.

> . . . .

> Who by aspersions throw a stone
> At th' head of others, hit their own.

28. See Wilcox, *The English Poems*, 347, where she cites Lull (*The Poem in Time*, 115–16) and Bloch (*Spelling the Word*, 187) along this line.

29. This phrase is Wilcox's summary of Freer's discussion of the poem in *Music for a King*, 139.

30. Ray suggests that "increasing admiration through the century for poets relying heavily on the couplet (e.g., Dryden, Cowley, Waller, and Denham) undoubtedly heightened the appeal of those poems by Herbert in which couplets play an important part" (5).

Who looks on ground with humble eyes,
Findes himself there, and seeks to rise.

When th' hair is sweet through pride or lust,
The powder doth forget the dust.

Wilcox finds the poem much about adopting "the example of the poor" in regard to humility (ll. 3–4) and the recognition that all humans are dust (ll. 11–14);[31] the poem's injunctions about giving to the needy and casting no aspersions are classic reminders about doing unto others what one would have done to oneself. These are matters of concern for the health of society—not just for the spiritual elevation or superiority of an individual.

But despite their high rank in seventeenth-century British allusion-making from Herbert's work, these two poems, "Content" and "Charms and Knots," are hardly the pinnacle of Herbert's social-justice (or social-levelling) expressions. For that experience, we must study a poem that probably puzzled and troubled many of its seventeenth-century readers theologically and that probably posed difficult imaginative challenges for some of them as well: "Humilitie." According to Ray's accounting of about 175 seventeenth-century writers, it is not the least cited of Herbert's poems, but I suppose that it may have suffered in its own time from some of "the apparent neglect of the metaphysically crafted and currently admired 'The Pulley' and 'The Windows,'" both of which Ray finds cited only once in the seventeenth century.[32] It is also possible that, as the century went on, "Humilitie" may have been seen as so contemporaneously political-by-allegory that it became a piece of yesterday's news about court and market corruption from the 1620s.[33] Whatever the case, it seems an intriguing possibility that the poem may be more dramatically a part of Herbert's biblically resonant psalter than has been thought.

---

31. Wilcox, *The English Poems*, 348–49, notes 3–4, 11–12, and 14.

32. Ray, Herbert's *Seventeenth-Century Reputation*, 3.

33. Sidney Gottlieb argues that the animating perspective of "Humilitie" is the recognition that "the Jacobean court was a place of graft and confusion" ("Herbert's Political Allegory," 471).

Chapter 2

"All the foundations of the earth are out of course"

Herbert's Mythopoeic Refraction of Psalm 82

OF THE RELATIVELY SMALL number of Herbert's poems that could plausibly be said to be primarily about biblical social concern, the one most heavily saturated with it seems to have received little attention for that feature. Although it has attracted commentators by its contemporary satiric and allegorical potential, "Humilitie" has been little, if at all, linked to the Psalms, which is a rich repository of Hebrew expressions of social concern. Using the KJV, Wilcox finds possible biblical intertextuality with Isa 6:1 ("I saw also the Lord sitting upon a throne, high and lifted up"), Rev 4:2 ("behold, a throne was set in heaven, and one sat on the throne"), and Job 35:11 ("[God] teacheth us more than the beasts of the earth, and maketh us wiser than the fowls of heaven"), but she uses those passages for strictly local comments on a few lines (1–3). Of the three passages, Rev 4 may be the best biblical analog because of its similar dramatic situation; however, if "The Church" is Herbert's psalter, the Vision of John is a strange place to look for analogs. I suggest that "Humilitie" has a nearer relationship to Psalm 82, a poem that, like "Humilitie," has no peer in its own collection and that has been similarly difficult for scholars to categorize.

I have found no scholarly claims of the two poems' manifest or constitutive intertextuality. Nevertheless, the extravagance of Herbert's allegory and its setting, if nothing else, should alert us to the possibility if we really take "The Church" to be his psalter and if we acknowledge the heavy influence that the Book of Psalms had upon him. Within some boundaries of reasonable correlation, I believe that we can find refracted elements of Psalm 82 in the Herbert poem. The major differentials in "Humilitie" may be seen as the most severe refractions of the Hebrew text—certain absences, for example, having the weight of presence. As far as social-concern elements go, "Humilitie" seems to be the poem most laden with them in "The Church." It may also be one of the most heavily refracted psalm-poems in an artistic sense.

PSALMIC CATEGORY OF THE POEMS: PSALM 82

Translations and paraphrases of Psalm 82 differ enough to make interpretation problematic, but let us give our attention to the Authorized Version (the KJV) of 1611 that Herbert would have known:

Psalm 82

1 God standeth in the congregation of the mighty; he judgeth among the gods.

2 How long will ye judge unjustly, and accept the persons of the wicked? Selah.

3 Defend the poor and fatherless: do justice to the afflicted and needy.

4 Deliver the poor and needy: rid them out of the hand of the wicked.

5 They know not, neither will they understand; they walk on in darkness: all the foundations of the earth are out of course.

6 I have said, Ye are gods; and all of you are children of the most High.

7 But ye shall die like men, and fall like one of the princes.

8 Arise, O God, judge the earth: for thou shalt inherit all nations.

Early-twentieth-century Bible scholar Hermann Gunkel places Psalm 82 in one of his seven minor types of psalms, the *liturgy*, which he considers a mixed-genre, antiphonal development out of earlier practices.[1] His main qualification for the category (an exceedingly simple one) is that a poem have a change of persona, or speaker, within it; of course, Psalm 82 is well known for having at least two, if not three, such changes. Here is the minimal case:

1. A narrator opens the poem-drama *in medias res*. God is already standing in council "among the gods" (KJV).[2]

1. On the minor genre, see *Introduction*, 19–20; on Ps 82 as liturgy, see 317.

2. With rare exceptions, other renderings of the scene tend to keep us at the mythological limin: "among gods" (1599 Geneva); "in the midst of the gods" (1989 NRSV); "in the midst of the gods" (2007 Alter); "among the 'gods'" (2011 NIV). The Wycliffe-Purvey (1388 WYC) version actually underscores the text's mythological liminality by an emphasis in the second clause: "God stood in the synagogue of gods; forsooth he deemeth gods in the middle." Even the highly conservative Holman version (2009 HCSB), created under the explicit ideal of biblical inerrancy, uses the phrase "among the gods"; and so does the NIV, with qualifying quotation marks around the word *gods*, apparently to suggest a figurative quality to the word. The 1995 NASB, generally considered a quite literal translation, seems to be an exception, giving us the phrase "in the midst of the rulers," but the accompanying footnote reads: "Lit[erally:] *gods*." The late return to literality suggests that the makers of the NASB decided that an *interpretive* puzzle-piece had to be inserted in order to make vv. 2–5 make sense. Further puzzlement awaits, however, in the NASB v. 6, where no apology is made for use of the statement "You are gods." If that is simply hyperbole, the explanation about dying "like men" and falling "like one of the princes" seems to be stating the obvious about mere mortals rather than pronouncing a severe penalty upon beings having no expectation of it. All together, the preponderance of translations brings us back to the mythopoeic boundary by allowing the unsettling possibility of multiple supernatural entities with more-than-angelic hegemonies in Psalm 82.

In completing the psalter her brother Philip had begun, the Countess of Pembroke (Mary Sidney Herbert), takes thirty lines/verses to render the eight verses of Ps 82 into metrically complex English poetry. Her version of 82:1 identifies the "gods" as human beings: "Where poor men plead at princes' bar, / Who gods (as God's viceregents) are: / The God of gods hath his tribunal pight [pitched], / Adjudging right / Both to the judge, and judgèd wight." Later, in her version of 82:7 (her line 23), she emphasizes the point: "But err not, princes: you as men must die" (*The Sidney Psalter*, 160–61).

2. The narrator's voice gives way to God's without introduction of the change. Depending upon the translation and any editorial pointing of the text with quotation marks or some other signs, God is quoted for at least two verses (6–7) and as many as six (2–7).[3]

3. The narrator resumes speaking at some point. Most versions of the text bring the narrator back in after God's pronouncement of judgment upon the malfeasant "gods." If the narrator is considered a worship leader, it is possible to consider verse 8 a corporately intoned *desideratum* and a request for God's continued rulership over all the nations. That is apparently Gunkel's reasoning in calling the psalm a liturgy.

Gunkel's "liturgy" classification does not distinguish a psalm (or a category) by its topics, so it is not very helpful in that regard. At one point, Gunkel does specifically use Psalm 82 as an example of the

3. The main problem in deciding how many verses are spoken by God is posed by the difficulty in determining the antecedent of "They" in v. 5. If it is "the gods," then v. 5 can hardly be part of God's speech; otherwise, he would be referring to his present second-person audience by a third-person pronoun. If the antecedent of "They" is the host of "lowly," "wretched," "poor," and needy" people named in vv. 3–4, then v. 5 can plausibly be placed in God's mouth. It is also possible that, as the NRSV has it, the narrator or another unnamed person speaks v. 5, referring to the "wretched" oppressed as those who "walk around in darkness." If that is the case in v. 5, we have a second change of speaker there, followed possibly by a third in vv. 6–7 and a fourth in v. 8. The NRSV reading gives us this sequence: Narrator (v. 1), God (2–4), Narrator (5), Narrator or God (6–7), Narrator (8). The NASB has the following: Narrator (1–5), God (6–7), Narrator (8). Alter (2007) reads the psalm thus: Narrator (1), God (2–7), Narrator (8). All three of those translations use quotation marks to show changes of speaker. The Authorized Version (KJV) does not use quotation marks, but like Alter's translation, it sets vv. 1 and 8 off from 2–7 in a manner that suggests a narrative-voice frame enclosing the words of God to the subordinate "gods": thus, Narrator (1), God (2–7), Narrator (8). In a descriptive heading, the 1599 Geneva Bible (GNV) attributes all of the words of the psalm to "the Prophet" (notice the sequence of verbs that seem to have "The Prophet" as their subject): "*1 The Prophet declaring God to be present among the Judges and Magistrates, 2 Reproveth their partiality. 3 And exhorteth them to do justice. 5 But seeing none amendment, 8 he desireth God to undertake the matter and execute justice himself.*" By Gunkel's criterion of multiple speakers, apparently the 1599 Geneva Bible's version of Ps 82 does not qualify as a General Liturgical poem. For my purposes in this paper, it is more important that the 1599 GNV does not provide a *dramatic* antecedent for Herbert's dramatic "Humilitie."

"prophetic judgment speech against all the heathen gods,"[4] but even that designation (or explanation) does not refer to any reasons why heathen gods are being punished. The interior lines of Psalm 82 do give a reason in the context of its particular dramatic situation, of course: the "gods" cited there, heathen or not, have not been faithful to their charges of establishing justice and moral order in the world. The most important topic of the psalm, however, is not a distinction between paganism and the worship of Yahweh; it is the malfeasance of subordinates in delegated governance.[5] God himself, the primary speaker in the poem, identifies that as his topic over vv. 2–5. In fact, God's social concerns are the reasons for the impending demotion. Their causal role is no reduction of their thematic importance *vis à vis* the disposition of the erstwhile "gods." Furthermore, the narrator-persona's respectful exhortation to God in v. 8 is a plea for God's taking over the role he had delegated to the lesser "gods." The dismissal of the other "gods" opens a social-concern (social governance) absence that the presence of the true God can fill with perfect and complete authority.

Interestingly, the malefactors in Psalm 82 are not allowed to speak in their own defense. Perhaps the phrase "How long" at the opening of v. 2 ("How long will you judge unjustly") is a sign that the whole sorry mismanagement situation has been going on under the eye of God to a point past defense in the authorities' blatant refusal to obey their original commission. Nevertheless, the "gods" apparently have a persistent mission that they must fulfill even under sentence of death. God's imperatives in vv. 3–4 are not references to an earlier commission; they have the simple force of ongoing requirement:

4. Gunkel, *Introduction*, 317.

5. Robert Alter agrees that "the poem is concerned with the infuriating preponderance of injustice in the world," but he also thinks that the psalm's "frankly mythological [. . .] character" is reason to understand the poem "[a]lternatively" as "rudely demot[ing]" the patron gods of nations other than Israel (*The Book of Psalms*, 293n8b). Gunkel sees it in the latter light, too, and it is reasonable to suppose that the ancient Israelites using Ps 82 would have made that assumption as well. My claim about "the malfeasance of subordinates in delegated governance" is based in the psalm's evident suggestion that God had given the lesser gods the chance to show their intents and abilities to govern well. Even with the understanding that the suggestion is a fictive "supposal," it is clear that the highest-level concern in the psalm is over the behavior (or lack of behavior) of the lesser gods rather than over the question of their existence.

3   Defend the poor and fatherless: do justice to the afflicted
     and needy.
4   Deliver the poor and needy: rid them out of the hand of the
     wicked. (KJV)

These imperatives seem to be a renewal of the "Go thou and do"
requirement that had been part of the original charters. Apparently
the demoted "gods" must carry on *in righteousness* under the new
dispensation of God's own direct governance in human affairs.

In Gunkel's terms, then, Psalm 82 is a "Judgment" poem in a
mixed liturgical mode. Bellinger considers it part of the "Elohistic"
Collection of the Psalter. He classifies it under "Praise," but, some-
what like Gunkel, subclassifies it under "Hymns with Prophetic
Warnings," along with Palms 50 and 81.[6] These category-names
do not suggest specific topical qualifications for inclusion, but the
subcategory names ("Judgment" and "Hymns with Prophetic Warn-
ings") well represent God's attitude in 82:2–7 toward those who ne-
glect and oppress the weak and the poor.

If Claus Westermann's simple binary classification were used,
we would have a hard time deciding whether Psalm 82 is a praise
poem or a lament.[7] Although verses 1 and 8 frame the poem in an
"incipient praise" modality, verses 2–7, its dramatic core, qualifies as
lament in two important ways: (a) it names and describes the chaos
into which the human world has fallen (vv. 2–5), and (b) it narrates
Yahweh's apparent disappointment over the irresponsible behavior of
those to whom the proper operation of the world has been entrusted.
In terms of the bulk, or volume, of its material, Psalm 82 seems to be
a lament or a veiled imprecation (against the irresponsible "gods");
in terms of its frame, it is something like a basis for praise, if not
exactly praise itself. In Brueggemann's widely recognized terms, the
frame refers to a condition of "orientation," of cosmological stabil-
ity; the interior of the poem refers to profound and widespread
"disorientation."[8] Technically, Psalm 82 does not end with new, or
restored, orientation, for only the *request* for God's administration

6. Bellinger, *Psalms*, 23.

7. Westermann, *Praise and Lament*, Part One ("The Categories of the
Psalms"), esp. 31 and 34; cited in Bellinger, *Psalms*, 22. See also Gunkel on
mixed categories, especially on praise and prophecy (*The Psalms*, 36–37).

8. Brueggemann, *Message*, 19–21.

of justice is dramatized. The new order(ing) has not yet begun; it is only adumbrated, hoped for, imagined under the rule of God. The end of the psalm is actually a kind of "investiture" or "coronation" speech-act that acknowledges the sovereignty of God. In that respect, Psalm 82 is much like an Enthronement Psalm, in Gunkel's terms, or, less precisely, a Royal Psalm, in Bellinger's terms.[9] Thus Psalm 82 is further difficult to classify.

PSALMIC CATEGORY OF THE POEMS: "HUMILITIE"

Concerns about cosmological stability and rulership, as well as the difficulty in categorizing the poem, will also be useful in our discussion of Herbert's "Humilitie":

> I Saw the Vertues sitting hand in hand
> In sev'rall ranks upon an azure throne,
> Where all the beasts and fowls by their command
> Presented tokens of submission.
> Humilitie, who sat the lowest there
>> To execute their call,
> When by the beasts the presents tendred were,
>> Gave them about to all.

9. In presenting his "Classification of the Psalms," Bellinger expresses his indebtedness to Gunkel and Westermann. Bellinger defines the psalms in Gunkel's "Enthronement" category as "hymns [that] celebrate the kingship of God," and he notes particularly two psalms that resonate well with verse 8 of Psalm 82: "Psalm 47 celebrates God's sovereign kingship over all the earth. Psalm 93 describes God's rule over the chaotic powers that bring disorder to the earth" (*Psalms*, 18). Both Gunkel and Bellinger use the term *Royal Psalm* to refer to psalms dealing with the needs, rights, and responsibilities of human kings. Bellinger comments that "[h]ope for the future seems to be the primary reason royal texts were included in the Psalter" (*Psalms*, 108). Verse 8 of Psalm 82 conveys a sense of that hopefulness. In discussing the conclusions of the psalms of lament, Bellinger comments that "[i]n most cases, [. . .] the crisis seems still to be present, though there is a kind of pause before the transition—in anticipation of a word from God" (55). The conclusion of Psalm 82 seems to match that description.

The angrie Lion did present his paw,
Which by consent was giv'n to Mansuetude.
The fearfull Hare her eares, which by their law
Humilitie did reach to Fortitude.
The jealous Turkie brought his corall-chain;
That went to Temperance.
On Justice was bestow'd the Foxes brain,
Kill'd in the way by chance.

At length the Crow bringing the Peacocks plume,
(For he would not) as they beheld the grace
Of that brave gift, each one began to fume,
And challenge it, as proper to his place,
Till they fell out: which when the beasts espied,
They leapt upon the throne;
And if the Fox had liv'd to rule their side,
They had depos'd each one.

Humilitie, who held the plume, at this
Did weep so fast, that the tears trickling down
Spoil'd all the train: then saying, *Here it is*
For which ye wrangle, made them turn their frown
Against the beasts: so joyntly bandying,
They drive them soon away;
And then amerc'd them, double gifts to bring
At the next Session-day.

Like Psalm 82, "Humilitie" is hard to categorize simply, unless one is content to call it an allegory, a beast fable, or a veiled satire. Unlike Psalm 82, it clearly does not seem to be, in Gunkel's biblical-studies terms, a liturgy, especially not of antiphonal variety. This should not be surprising within the extant work of a churchman-poet who eschewed writing metrical psalms for congregational singing even though his talents were probably up to the task. At a stretch, perhaps the narrative poem could be considered a catechistic anecdote suitable for delivery as part of a homily's *exordium* or *confirmatio*, but its thickly allegorical surface makes the poem better suited for unstructured meditation than liturgy. That, too, seems to make the poem fit well within Herbert's generally meditative collection.

Critical readings of "Humilitie" in the past few decades have been greatly diverse. John R. Mulder calls it one of a number of "methodological studies" in *The Temple* in which Herbert's persona attempts to "trace designs" in some domain of study but "is baffled by an apparent contrast in the evidence."[10] Although Mulder does not analyze "Humilitie" closely, it would seem that the poem's main "contrast" or ambiguity is in the Virtues' venality. The relative ease with which they are moved to greed and eventually to heavy-handed use of power compromises their stature as vice-regents of their allegorical domain. Mulder counts "Humilitie" among at least nine poems in "The Church" that pose *dilemmas* rather than answers or solutions.[11] In this regard, Mulder seems to recognize that all of the loose ends are not tied up in "Humilitie."

Richard Strier thinks the poem more complete in its redemptive and catechistic operations. He considers "Humilitie" a mixed, or dual, allegory having (a) social and (b) psychological/spiritual tenors.[12] He finds it "Herbert's most considered statement on ethical humanism" but also a deeply psychomachic poem with strong Calvinist overtones about the operation of grace in the life of a "regenerate Christian." Strier seems to consider "Humilitie" on the whole a *solution* poem, commenting that "stanza 4 depicts the restoration of order in the soul through the entrance of Humility into the action." Notice that, for Strier, the solution quality of the poem seems to reside in the psychomachic interpretative option, not in the broad-social-sphere option. Strier indicates that mere humanist virtue cannot long or alone hold the beastly Passions at bay, and he concludes that "the humanist claim for the virtues"—that they have

---

10. Mulder, "*The Temple* as Picture," 8.

11. Mulder's list may not be exhaustive by his analysis, but he names the following as "dilemma" or "baffle[ment]" poems: "Humilitie," "The World," "Sion," "Providence," "The Storm," "Paradise," "The Method," "Artillerie," and "Josephs coat" (8).

12. Strier, "Ironic Humanism," 46–50. The descriptive terms *mixed* and *dual* are mine, not Strier's.

permanently subjugated the beasts—is "false."[13] In Strier's analysis, then—although he does not say so explicitly—"Humilitie" has both satiric and homiletic functions corresponding respectively to the two allegorical readings. Applying Walter Brueggemann's terms to Strier's discussion, *disorientation* comes to be the systemic condition of the plenary world but *new orientation* the systemic condition of the regenerate soul. Humility produced and strengthened by grace becomes the agent of re-orientation that provides a psychomachic solution to the anarchy of the Passions. Obviously, such a reading of the poem would be attractive to Arminians because it locates the instrumentality and objective reality of social improvement in the individual regenerate soul.

Sidney Gottlieb has influentially argued that "Humilitie" is a satire on the corrupt political-patronage system of Herbert's time, one of a group of poems in close *Temple* proximity that Gottlieb calls "a 'contempt of court' sequence": "Content," "The Quidditie," "Humilitie," "Frailtie," and "Constancie" (numbers 61–65 in Wilcox's 2007 edition of Herbert's English poems).[14] To suspect Herbert of such an intention or application is not at all hard to support with what we know of his failed (or set aside) political ambitions, but even Gottlieb considers his argument just an expansion of the poem's potentials, not a contradiction of Strier's satire-on-humanism argument or of Joseph Summers's comments upon the efficacy of Humility to control the natural passions in the human psyche.[15] Indeed, given the rich multivalence and productive ambiguity of most of the poems in the collection, a narrowly political understanding of "Humilitie" seems too restrictive. If, in fact, "The Church" is Herbert's psalter, the biblical precedent suggests that many, if not most, poems should be meaningful on more than one level—generally not to exclude the anagogical (or spiritual/theological). "The Church" clearly exemplifies spiritual reflection and invites the reader's theological excursions.

---

13. Strier, "Ironic Humanism," 48.

14. Gottlieb, "Herbert's Political Allegory," 477. Wilcox calls special attention to Gottlieb's argument in her introduction to "Humilitie" in *The English Poems*, 256.

15. Summers, *George Herbert*, 172.

Along that line, Roger B. Rollin classifies "Humilitie" as a "Sacred Poem" having "public," "doctrinal," and "didactic" characteristics.[16] Similarly, Stanley Fish argues that *The Temple* is Herbertian catechism rendered in "homiletic mode."[17] Mulder calls the collection "a controlled dramatization and [. . .] a critique and reenactment of the religious life." Further, he states that "one's understanding of the Christ figure is the implied norm in *The Temple*."[18] Marion White Singleton claims that the "courtly ideal" poems from "Content" through "Constancie" (which include "Humilitie") are actually exercises in "adding the distinctive values of Christianity" to the "traditional virtues" in order to "make up the virtues' insufficiencies."[19] These and many other critics' discussions of *The Temple* have constructed a broad consensus that its theological and spiritual aspects are of primary importance in understanding the collection; thus, Gottlieb's political argument, however correct, may actually serve to explain the vehicle of a metaphor whose tenor has to do with a broader social concern—i.e., may add concrete basis for an allegorical interpretation.

Like Psalm 82, "Humilitie" is a mixed-genre allegorical poem with significant social-concern characteristics. Helen Vendler finds it "allegorically predictable and therefore uninteresting," but she also identifies its "unhappy ending" as a sign of Herbert's ironic capacity and of his willingness to experiment with given poetic forms.[20] Perhaps his experimentation ran to a heavily refracted re-envisioning of Psalm 82, which, ironically, represents the only one of Bellinger's psalm-categories that has no "hits" in Wilcox's accounting of Herbert's psalmic allusions.

16. Rollin, "Self-Created Artifact," 158. Rollin apparently does not see or find important the psychomachic aspect of the poem that Strier sees.

17. Reported by Mulder in "*The Temple* as Picture," 13n3.

18. Mulder in "*The Temple* as Picture," 13n3.

19. Singleton, *God's Courtier*, 176.

20. In finding the ending of the poem "unhappy," Vendler, like Mulder, differs from Strier.

THE FRAMES OF THE POEMS

Psalm 82 and "Humilitie" both open with a fictive surprise that requires suspension of disbelief: the persona claims to give us an eyewitness picture of events happening in the divine realm (or on the boundary between the human and the divine), which is populated at least partly by mythological and/or mythopoeic figures. The openings are similar enough and different enough to be fascinating:

Psalm 82	"Humilitie"
1 God standeth in the congregation of the mighty; he judgeth among the gods. (KJV)	Lines 1–4: I saw the Vertues sitting hand in hand In sev'rall ranks upon an azure throne, Where all the beasts and fowls by their command Presented tokens of submission.

Because Psalm 82 has a distinct mythological aspect—Yahweh pictured dramatically in v. 1 as standing among the gods in "divine council" (NRSV)—some Christian readers may marginalize its importance because it seems to be of a kind with many ancient Near Eastern texts, particularly Mesopotamian and Ugaritic examples, regarding pagan deities.[21] Its liminality in that respect has probably prevented it from being frequently used for corporate worship and homiletic purposes in Christian churches that do not use all of the psalms in liturgical rotation throughout the year. Readers who suspend disbelief, however, are given privileged seats for an intensely compacted drama featuring God as judge or prosecutor of the other divine figures, "the mighty." His standing position probably represents his having risen in dismay and/or anger from a seated position, leaving his audience seated below him. Since He is apparently doing the judging, it is not convincing to consider him a mere prosecutor, but he has dramatically "unenthroned" himself (stepped out of his seat or off his throne) to act decisively in a matter of great moment. The other members of the council, the vice-regent "gods," remain

---

21. But see Trotter, "Death of the אלהים in Psalm 82," esp. 228–33, where he argues that the subordinate "gods" named in the psalm are neither supernatural entities nor "human judicial officials" but rather "divine kings" (228), by which term he means "human kings who were considered to have divine status" (233).

silent throughout the drama. Reduced to voicelessness, they are dis-
empowered and subdued.

"Humilitie" also presents a problematic mythopoeic liminal-
ity, but its valence is not as immediately troublesome, theologically,
as that of Psalm 82. The Judeo-Christian God is not in evidence, at
least by name, although Christian typologists/interpreters/readers
have assumed that Herbert's addition of Humility to the pantheon
of humanist virtues is based in his considering it a quintessentially
Christian trait. Singleton, for example, explicitly connects Humility's
behaviors to those of Christ in the latter's "relinquish[ment] of the
world,"[22] and Joseph Summers simply calls Humility "the fifth and
Christian virtue" in the poem,[23] notwithstanding the fact that ancient
Greek culture and later emulators recognized humility as a form or
subclass of Temperance, one of the other four Virtues in Herbert's
poem. Surely Herbert would have known of that classification, so his
choice to give Humility its own seat upon the jointly held but rank-
ordered "azure throne" is interesting. It may simply reflect his close
and constant reading of Scripture, which presented him in many
places with the directives that have raised humility to the rank of a
Christian virtue (for example, Phil 2:1–17, Jas 4:6, and 1 Pet 5:5). One
verse having particular resonance with the poem is Phil 2:3 (KJV):
"Let nothing be done through strife or vainglory; but in lowliness
of mind let each esteem other better than themselves."[24] In fact, the
verse might be considered a perfect Aesopian moral for the poem.

Herbert's refracted "congregation of the mighty" turns out to be
the pantheon of ethical humanist Virtues with the somewhat redun-
dant addition of Humility and with the substitution of Mansuetude
(meekness, gentleness) for Prudence. Here the liminal discomfort
is a matter of the poem's universe seeming to have only the Virtues
as supreme authority and power and therefore a less transcendent

22. Singleton, *God's Courtier*, 178. This seems to suggest that Singleton un-
derstands the character Humility to be a masculine figure in Herbert's drama.
See also 243n17, where Singleton sees Humility's offer of the plume to all of the
Virtues as "an echo of Christ's humble sacrifice."

23. Summers, *George Herbert*, 172.

24. Wilcox does not list this verse in her discussion of "Humilitie," nor
does she list the poem as one of those in *The Temple* that refer to the Book of
Philippians.

source of Righteousness. Thus the poem opens with a view of a complacent Christian or Neostoicist humanism confident in its own hegemonic right and powers. Interestingly, though, the Virtues are seated in ranks; thus, at the beginning of the narrative, we see an emblem of their susceptibility to pride that Humility will critique by acting as servant of all.[25] Such behavior, of course, makes a Christian reader's easy identification of Humility with Christ almost inevitable.

Like the frame-persona of Psalm 82, the narrative persona in "Humilitie" gives us a "congregation of the mighty" in the heavenlies: "the Vertues sitting hand in hand / In sev'rall ranks upon an azure throne," but these mighty humanist ideals are "sitting" in state, "hand in hand," as if unperturbed about any particular state of affairs and as if in satisfied certainty of their own divine equilibrium and the orderly operation of their demesne. If Herbert had Psalm 82 in his ear, these seem to be foreboding refractions. First, whatever the state of affairs in the jurisdiction of the Virtues, the rulers apparently see and hear no evil as long as the tribute comes in. They have gathered in stately session to receive gifts from subjects whom they apparently consider sufficiently cowed to remain harmless, whom they apparently do not suspect of imminent treason or anarchy. The power of the Virtues is perhaps such that they can "command" the presentation of such gifts—or at least can command the "beasts and fowls" to come forward in a certain order to make their presentations. In short, the opening situation in "Humilitie" is that of an apparently unthreatened hegemony of the Virtues.

It is also interesting that the Virtues, except for Humility, remain seated—that is, *inactive* as far as engagement with the needs of their subjects is concerned. The main "direction of activity" in the poem is that of the subjects' meeting the "needs" of the Virtues for respect and for acknowledgment of the Virtues' power. I suggest that this may be an ironized version of God's imperatives to the subordinate "gods" in Ps 82:3–4:

25. If a reader should object that the Virtues should not be expected to act "out of character" as regards their ranks, we need only point to Herbert's readily postulating that all but Humility are easily susceptible to greed and pride. We might consider this another of Herbert's refractions—this time of classical Western ethical theory.

3 Defend the poor and fatherless: do justice to the afflicted and needy.

4 Deliver the poor and needy: rid them out of the hand of the wicked.

In the biblical text, the superiors (the "gods") are enjoined to present gifts to the inferiors, so to speak—to do works of righteousness for the suffering. In Herbert's poem, the inferiors are commanded to present gifts to the superiors. In the biblical text, God *stands* among the sitting "gods" to act on behalf of the oppressed and needy; in Herbert's poem, the Virtues sit to receive gifts for themselves. They seem both indolent and self-satisfied.

THE "MAIN ACTION" OF THE DRAMA

THE MAIN DRAMA IS handled differently in the two poems. In Psalm 82, the plot is diachronically minimal but synchronically maximal. Everything comes to a halt for six verses (2–7) while the dramatic centerpiece, God's sentencing soliloquy, goes on. In "Humilitie," the plot gathers increasing diachronic momentum, act after act happening in quick succession, as if to represent the rampant chaos unleashed by Passions and peccant Virtues alike. Even Humility, the closest approximation to a truly Godlike being in the poem, limits his[26] soliloquy to a single despairing statement, *"Here it is / For which ye wrangle."*

26. Humility's gender is not made clear in the poem, but line 20 uses the masculine pronoun *his* to refer to all of the other Virtues ("each one began to fume, / And challenge it, as proper to his place"). Unless we were carelessly to consider Humility female only because (a) it sits "lowest" on the throne (line 5) or because (b) it "weep[s]" over the other Virtues' quarreling and greed, it seems best to accept Herbert's suggestion that all of the Virtues in his vision are male. Since weeping has stereotypically been thought to come less easily or quickly to males, Humility's sorrowful behavior in the last stanza may actually seem more profound for its supposed rarity if the character is male. If indeed, as Singleton repeatedly suggests, Humility is a stand-in for Christ, Herbert has certainly produced an echo of the weeping male Savior, whose emotional lability is considered an empathic criterion for Christians. Strier, too, has noticed Humility's gender ambiguity in the poem, referring in one place to "the hero (heroine?) of the poem" ("Ironic Humanism," 46); however, he does not answer the parenthetical question directly or indirectly (e.g., by using telling pronouns).

In Psalm 82, God's opening rhetorical question with its embedded charges (v. 2) is actually the second half of an ironic chiastic structure that connects the opening frame-member, verse 1, to God's discourse. The chiasm also provides the deontological backdrop for the peroration in vv. 6–7. In the following layout of vv. 1–2, the relationships of the "crossing" parallel terms are of contrastive sort, although that value becomes clearer in a recursive reading:

1   <u>God standeth in the congregation of the mighty</u>; he judgeth among the gods.

2   How long will ye judge unjustly, <u>and accept the persons of the wicked</u>? Selah.

The chiasm illuminates the following dynamics:

- **In 1a**, the narrator presents an angry God who rises to distinguish himself and his rules of order from the vice-regents who have not emulated him or followed his rules. **In 2b**, the misbehavior of the vice-regents is exactly what God will not do in regard to them; in other words, God himself will not "accept the persons of the wicked" in the forms of the vice-regents. He is about to perform the speech-acts to disenfranchise them.

- **In 1b**, God's proper expression of hegemony is set over against **2a**, the vice-regents' improper use of their delegated power.

Here is a more traditional layout and markup of the chiasm:

A   God standeth in the congregation of the mighty;

  B   he judgeth among the gods.

  B1   How long will ye judge unjustly,

A1   and accept the persons of the wicked? Selah.

The psalm's closing chiasm (in vv. 6–7) mirrors the ironies of the opening one:

> 6 I have said, Ye *are* gods; and all of you *are* children of the most High.
>
> 7 But ye shall die like men, and fall like one of the princes.

God's own ironic—even sardonic—tone is palpable as he begins his peroration and verdict/sentencing:

A I have said, Ye *are* gods;

　B and all of you are children of the most High.

　B1 But ye shall die like men

A1 and fall like one of the princes.

The psalmist represents God as disappointed and perhaps even surprised by the vice-regents' self-disqualification for immortality and, therefore, seats on the council. In terms of speech-act theory, God's earlier declaration "Ye are gods" seems in quotation to have lost its illocutionary and perlocutionary forces, for the "gods" seem (a) to have lost the sense that they are obligated to act in Godlike ways and (b) to have lost their immortality. God's frustration is reflected in v. 5, which figuratively describes chaos metastasizing from the realm of the metaphysical (epistemology) to that of the physical (phenomenology):

> 5 They know not, neither will they understand; they walk on in darkness:
>
> all the foundations of the earth are out of course.

God's quotation of his first declaration, however, becomes newly forceful in its ironic application: it is the measure of the vice-regents' failure to perform their constative roles; it is the criterion by which they have disqualified themselves for God's favor. That is to say: the word has not returned void after all.

I suggest that Herbert's "Humilitie" presents an imaginative view of the Psalm 82 vice-regents' own *council manqué* wherein a showy semblance of moral elevation without God's presence turns out to deconstruct itself. The poem essentially provides an imaginative exemplum of the sort of vice-regent behavior that angers God in Psalm 82. It is as if Herbert "fills in the gaps" of 82:2–6 with something like plausible narrative details *within a mythopoeic, allegorical mode.* In other words, Herbert's fictive "vision" plausibly extends the deontologically problematic force of 82:2–5 by concretizing the vice-regents' misbehavior in a refracted allegorical mode. I am reminded of C. S. Lewis's calling his Narnia books "supposals" for much the same reason, meaning that he had freed himself from common obligations to make rigidly rational and rigorously mimetic narratives with all the features of adult realism. The diachronic pressure of the plot in "Humilitie," which becomes syntactically more frenzied in the last two stanzas,[27] suggests a gathering, negative moral inertia, but the whole poem seems, in consideration of Herbert's soaking in the Psalter, to operate as a synchronic deepening of the reason for God's sentencing the vice-regents of Psalm 82 to mortality.

Herbert's poem, of course, has no punishment for the Virtues. By the end of the poem, they may have learned a lesson, but it seems not to be persistent in their memory or fully assimilated to their ethic, for they punish the Passions rather than themselves. In psychological terms, their action against the Passions seems to exhibit characteristics of several defense mechanisms: *projection, displacement,* and *overcompensation.* When Humility sorrowfully states about the ruined peacock plume, "*Here it is / For which ye wrangle*" (ll. 27–28), the quarrelling Virtues "turn their frown / Against the beasts."[28] The

---

27. Notice the radically different rhythms of the first two and the last two stanzas. In the first two, the orderliness of procedure is suggested by the periods at the ends of the sentences that divide the action into cycles of expected accomplishment: grammatical marking for rhetorical and performative "periods." Stanza 1 has two full sentences, each closed with a period. The sense of firm order is even greater in Stanza 2, whose quatrains are *punctuated* in couplets. With the beginning of the Virtues' feud, the narrative is rendered with an appropriately propulsive frenzy managed—or barely restrained—by commas, semicolons, and colons until a final period is reached. It seems important that Herbert did not end the poem with a stanza suggesting the recovery of order.

28. A fruitful ambiguity enters with Herbert's choice of the verb *made* in line 28: "Humilitie, [. . .] then saying, *Here it is / For which ye wrangle*, made them turn their frown / Against the beasts" (ll. 25–29). Does the verb represent (a) a sufficient speech-act accomplishment? Or does it suggest (b) a nonverbal constraint of some kind not described by the narrator-persona? Since Humilitie's statement is so irony-laden, it seems to be a strong rhetorical ploy to shame

"frown," we should realize, is an artifact of their own quarrel, in which "each one began to fume, / And challenge it [the plume] as proper to his place, / Till they fell out" (ll. 19–21). In refocusing their frown toward the Passions, the Virtues (a) reassign blame for the irruptive social chaos and (b) displace their anger at their peers onto the Passions. The severe sentence meted out upon the Passions—"double gifts to bring / At the next Session-day"—seems like overcompensation, particularly since it follows so close upon the implicit rebuke from Humility, the lowest among them.

Gottlieb, who reads "Humilitie" as a political satire about court life in Herbert's own time, looks askance at the earlier, more orderly, behaviors of the Virtues as well. He considers the beasts' gifts to be something like bribes approved and expected by the Virtues, and he notes the "grim" fact that "each of the gifts is [. . .] a body part, calling to mind a ritual of criminal punishment rather than that of voluntary and loving deference."[29] These observations and deductions are shrewd and sensible, and they can serve for my argument as well as for his. In the first place, Herbert's narrator characterizes the setting as a "Session-day" (l. 32), which makes it an assize-court (*criminal justice*) proceeding. If in fact the Passions are considered malefactors rather than tribute-bringers or tax-payers, the descriptive term is appropriate. But Scripture itself, which Herbert knew so well, makes prejudgment or full alienation of the Passions problematic. Bible readers are told to "be [. . .] angry and sin not" (Eph 4:26 [KJV]) as well as to "fear the Lord" (e.g., in Ps 33:8 and 34:9) and to "fear him [God] which is able to destroy both soul and body in hell" (Matt 10:28 [KJV]). God is characterized in at least sixteen passages as a "jealous" divinity (e.g., in Exod 34:14 and 2 Cor 11:2); and Mansuetude (Meekness, Gentleness) should recognize a close cousin in the Hare's Timidity. In "The Church-porch," lines 261–64, Herbert him-

---

the feuding Virtues and thus "make" them "turn their frown." That locution, ironized by the bedraggling of the plume, has the illocutionary force of an "offer" and the perlocutionary force of (a) reducing their interest in the plume, (b) shaming them, (c) redirecting their anger toward the beasts, (d) projecting blame upon the beasts, and (e) causing the feuding Virtues to "bandy together" (take up common cause). The end-of-poem events in lines 30–32 (the driving out and fining of the beasts) follow directly from that chain (or constellation) of perlocutionary forces.

29. Gottlieb, "Herbert's Political Allegory," 471–72.

self writes, "[S]uch jealousie / As hurts not others, but may make thee better, / Is a good spurre. Correct thy passions spite; / Then may the beasts draw thee to happy light." These are counsels of temperance, not annihilation. They are nuanced understandings of the Passions' utility under control. The Virtues in Herbert's poem, however, have an un-nuanced view of the Passions; they see no proper applications for the Passions' quintessences. It might be objected, here, that we are dealing with allegory and therefore with the inescapable generalization and stereotyping that characterizes the mode, but it is certainly possible to allegorize Individuality and Measured Behavior as well as Critical Thinking and Compassion. Herbert's Virtues seem to have prejudged the Passions to the point at which the latters' ritual maiming seems necessary even if no particular charges have been entered upon them.

Along that line, we should pause over Herbert's choices of Passions to populate the poem. Cicero's catalog of Stoic passions runs to thirty-two subcategories among its four main *genera* of disorder: Lust, Fear, Delight, and Distress.[30] If Herbert had intended to establish a thoroughly and radically anarchic cadre of Passions to threaten the Virtues in his poem, ones capable of fomenting violent rebellion and likely to do so, it would seem that he would have chosen more characters from the category of Lust, which includes Anger, Rage, Hate, Enmity, Wrath, Greed, and Longing. Indeed, he placed the "angrie Lion" and the mere memory of the recently deceased Fox in the poem; but the Hare, the "Turkie," and the probably absent Peacock represent passions from the categories of Fear, Distress, and Delight, respectively. Without underestimating the corruptive potential of those passions—for, after all, the Peacock's plume unhinges the Virtues—they seem not the most likely to stage a direct assault upon the very throne of the vice-regents. The Peacock, after all, may not be at the assize.[31] In a way, his place is taken by the Crow, who arrives with

30. These are J. E. King's translations from Cicero, *Tusculan Disputations* IV.vi.11–12 (p. 339). C. D. Yonge translates these "divisions of perturbations" as "Lust," "Fear," "Joy," and "Grief" (Cicero, *Cicero's Tusculan Disputations*, 296).

31. Many readers will probably find my qualification puzzling, for it is probably generally assumed that the Peacock itself is absent. The poem does not, however, completely extinguish the possibility that the Peacock is in attendance but simply unwilling to bring his plume up to the throne and the waiting hands of Humility. I admit that the scenario would require us to imagine either (a) a

"the Peacocks plume," but, even so, the balance of more-aggressive *vs.* less-aggressive Passions is fifty-fifty (Lion and Crow *vs.* Hare and Turkey). I suggest that the mix is not particularly promising for a throne-room uprising.

Timidity, for example, the Hare's quality, is a form, or expression, of the passion of Fear, which is not logically to be suspected of seeking opportunities for violent behavior. In *Tusculan Disputations,* Cicero defines Fear as "a belief of threatening evil which seems to the subject of it [the one who feels it] insupportable";[32] thus, the ironic notion of Pusillanimity's attacking hegemonic powers is hard to picture, and it would seem to deconstruct the very allegorical project it would support. It is classically significant, furthermore, that Herbert characterizes the timid Hare as a female in line 11.

Jealousy, the Turkey's quality, is a form of the passion of Distress, which is similarly not much to be suspected of violent sedition. According to Cicero, Jealousy is a "distress arising from the fact that the thing one has coveted oneself is in the possession of the other man as well as one's own."[33] Since, however, Cicero's definition of Distress in general is "a newly formed belief of present evil, *the subject of which thinks it right to feel depression and shrinking of soul,*"[34] the Turkey also seems an odd choice for violent anarchist.

The Peacock's quality, Pride (Cicero: "Ostentation"; "pleasure shown in outward demeanor and puffing oneself out extravagantly"[35]), is a form of the passion of Delight, by which term Cicero means a pathological attachment (or addiction) to pleasure. He defines Delight as a disorder of the soul arising from "a newly formed belief of present good," on which basis "the subject of it thinks it right to feel enraptured."[36] This definition would seem to account for the

---

dramatic Trickster theft by the Crow in the company of all or (b) a grudging allowance by the Peacock that the Crow may take the plume up to the Virtues. For the most part, I am content to believe that the Peacock is not in attendance. The main reason the possibility of the Peacock's presence is of interest to me is that his addition would give the less-aggressive beasts a majority and thus strengthen my argument about the causes of the uprising.

32. Cicero, *Tusculan Disputations,* 343 (IV.vii.14).

33. Cicero, *Tusculan Disputations,* 347 (IV.viii.18).

34. Cicero, *Tusculan Disputations,* 343 (IV.vii.14; my italics).

35. Cicero, *Tusculan Disputations,* 349 (IV.viii.20–21).

36. Cicero, *Tusculan Disputations,* 343 (IV.vii.14).

Peacock's prideful attachment to its plumage and its reticence to attend the assize or surrender its "plume." Wilcox remarks that "the peacock's conventional pride" prevents it from "lower[ing] itself sufficiently to offer a gift to the virtues."[37]

None of this is to say that the Passions may not "bandy together" as the Virtues do in driving them out near the end of Herbert's "Humilitie"; in fact, they do seem to act in unison if not in concert when they "[leap] upon the throne" (l. 22). My point, here, is that they are an odd band—lacking a leader, as we are told, since the Fox has been killed, and given opportunity only by the sensation raised by the Crow's arriving with the peacock's plume. Wilcox takes the phrase "the Crow bringing the Peacocks plume" (l. 17) to mean that the crow "hides its threatening blackness in a peacock's bright-coloured plumage,"[38] but the poem actually leaves certain things unclear: (a) whether the Crow brings the peacock's entire "tail" or just some part of it; (b) whether the Crow *wears* an array of plumage (such as the entire "tail") or just *carries* whatever plumage he has obtained. Line 27 does mention "the train," which may refer to the "tail." By picturing the Crow *dressed in* the plumage, Wilcox seems to have been influenced by Gottlieb's court-satire reading to consider the crow a figure of the "upstart courtier whose avarice caused the collapse of court etiquette in the Jacobean period."[39] As I have said, that reading is plausible on the sociohistorical level; however, Wilcox's reading of the Crow's disguise may be a "back formation" from Gottlieb's history.

As Wilcox notes, the Crow, of course, has allegorical resonances of "covetousness and ambition."[40] In Cicero's terms, the Crow may be said to express several types of passion: Greed (*genus*: LUST), Ostentation (DELIGHT), and Rivalry (DISTRESS); perhaps it is therefore enough of an instigator to move the Hare and the Turkey to insurrection. Like the Fox, archetypally, the Crow is a Trickster, known particularly for thieving; thus, we may suspect that Herbert's Crow has stolen the Peacock's plume. It is implausible that the Pea-

37. Wilcox, *The English Poems*, 258n18.

38. Wilcox, *The English Poems*, 258n17.

39. Wilcox, *The English Poems*, 258n17. Wilcox refers to Gottlieb's argument in "Herbert's Political Allegory," 474.

40. Wilcox, "Herbert's Political Allegory," 474.

cock would be any more willing to give up his plume to the Virtues because the Crow offers to bring it to the throne for him. The Crow's aggressiveness probably marks him as a less accomplished Trickster stand-in for the Fox.

Singleton claims in a long note that "the peacock's plume clearly does not represent only worldly pride. In the turn of the fable, it may indeed symbolize the gift of Christ to man."[41] Her argument is based upon the fact that "in Christian iconography the peacock also represented the Resurrection."[42] Although she admits that "Herbert is surely referring to the plume as a sign of worldly pride, an exterior show," she puzzlingly substitutes the following anagogical interpretation:

> [I]f the plume, when rightly understood in its spiritual significance, symbolizes the Resurrection, the action of Humilitie in giving it to all, as an echo of Christ's humble sacrifice, translates the gift to a spiritual one which rightly strengthens rather than divides the harmonious rule of the Virtues [. . .]. [I]t is Humilitie [not the peacock] who offers this gift which restores rule to the Virtues and renews the harmony destroyed by their wrangling.[43]

This analysis is hopeful, but the poem itself does not support it well, if at all. In the first place, Humility does not really give the bedraggled plume as a gift; he holds it up as an emblem of the other Virtues' cupidity. "*Here it is,*" he says, "*For which ye wrangle.*" The chastisement in the statement is palpable. In speech-act terms, Humility's constative locution has an illocutionary force of blame and a perlocutionary force of frustrating, even angering, the other Virtues. The other Virtues' "frown" is a sign of unanimous displeasure over each one's failure to acquire the unsullied plume. The tears of Humility, in fact, have "Spoil'd all the train." It is indeed difficult to see any reason why the sodden object of vanity should be interpreted as a sign of bright new birth in "Humilitie." The poem does not explain what happens to the peacock's plume after the beasts are driven away, but the very

41. Singleton, *God's Courtier*, 244n17. See also n. 16 and the rest of n. 17 on p. 243.

42. Singleton, *God's Courtier*, 243n16.

43. Singleton, *God's Courtier*, 243–44n17.

lack of further mention suggests that it is no longer of interest to the Virtues. This absence, too, does not comport well with the "Resurrection" idea, unless the absence is an ironic emblem of humanist disinterest in old-fashioned religious sentiment. Such an argument would seem too convoluted to me.

Wilcox pauses over the word *grace* in line 18, calling it "[p]rimarily a reference to the elegance of the peacock's plumage, a worldly sense of 'grace'"; but she also agrees with Richard Strier in calling it a "crucial reminder of divine grace which alone has the capacity," in Strier's words, to "'eradicate pride and truly to control the passions.'"[44] I have no objection to the reminder, but its force is almost completely enervated by the last stanza of the poem, which is highly ironic in its suggestion that order has been restored. The order, restored or newly amplified, is a rule of vindictive hegemony that seems not to understand the concept of any legitimate operation of the passions, psychomachically or socially. In other words, ironically Temperance does not seem to be very effective in the council of the virtues at the end of the poem. In C. D. Yonge's translation of the *Tusculan Disputations*, Cicero says of temperance, "I do not know whether that virtue may not be properly called frugality," a virtue whose "peculiar property seems to be, to govern and appease all tendencies to too eager a desire after anything, to restrain lust, and to preserve a decent steadiness in everything. The vice in contrast to this is called prodigality."[45] Given that the tribute already required of the beasts has been body parts, one wonders what "double gifts" might mean in line 31. Will the "fearfull Hare" now be required to give up her two front paws after already having lost her ears? Is this not an emblem of ferocious exaction of vengeance? The Virtues in Herbert's poem seem to be as prodigal, as intemperate, in their sentencing as in their internecine quarreling.

The closing of the narrative frame in "Humilitie" is altogether *not* a happy matter. The Virtues are almost as discomfited as the beasts. Humility, weepingly sorrowful, is just gathering himself after narrowly averting defeat by showing the ruined object of the other Virtues' illicit hopes; the others are bitterly vindictive and so recently

44. Wilcox, *The English Poems*, 258n18.

45. Cicero, *Cicero's Tusculan Disputations*, 98–99 (III.viii).

alienated from their peers that the atmosphere is deeply strained. Whereas Strier sees the operation of grace in the poem "to eradicate pride and truly to control the passions in man,"[46] I see a graceless-ness of *rulers manqué* whose own culpability is partly to blame for the chaos that has arisen. Whereas Singleton sees "a restoration of harmony" in the world of the allegory, I see a situation that has gone from bad to worse.[47] The doubled fine levied against the beasts does not seem like the work of Humility; it seems, as I have said earlier, like the work of heavily defended personalities seeking to displace or project blame elsewhere. "Herbert's poet," says Mulder, "reaches no further [in "Humilitie"] than the dilemma that is restated in *"Providence"* [sic]: He is baffled by an apparent contrast in the evidence." This bafflement seems to be Helen Vendler's to some extent, too, and it would be mine if I were not to suspect that "Humilitie" is Herbert's Psalm 82—a refraction of the biblical drama-poem that postulates a fictional incident in plausible accordance with the vice-regents' misbehaviors in the psalm. Calling attention to the wide variety of personae in *The Temple*, Patrides credits Herbert with "a natural inclination to dramatize in order to achieve an optimum of tonal range."[48] To this I would add "an optimum of scriptural catechism, sometimes to the extent of social or theological subversion or at least defamiliarization."

Verse 5 of Psalm 82 is a particularly interesting pericope in regard to linkages between the psalm and "Humilitie." In that verse, those who "walk on in darkness," knowing and understanding nothing, are generally thought to be common human beings—the poor, fatherless, afflicted, needy—who have been given short shrift by the vice-regent "gods." The history of the psalm's translation, however, calls that identification into question. Translators and interpreters must decide who is speaking to whom in the passage, and apparently

46. Strier, "Ironic Humanism," 49.

47. Sidney Gottlieb observes that "[w]e are accustomed to noting reversals, underminings, conclusions in which nothing is concluded, and backslidings in Herbert's most profoundly personal and introspective poems; it should come as no surprise to find these qualities in his more public, political poems as well" ("Herbert's Political Allegory," 475).

48. Patrides, *Figures in a Renaissance Context*, 134.

the Hebrew text does not make it easy. The Authorized Version has it as follows:

> 5 They know not, neither will they understand; they walk
> on in darkness [. . .].

Some English versions point the entire psalm with quotation marks in order to clarify the rhetorical situation. At least three different possibilities have been suggested. Most versions seem to take for granted that God is speaking to the assembled "gods" in vv. 2–7 but that "they" in v. 5 refers to the common human beings who have been ignored or made victims of injustice by the vice-regents (vv. 2–4). The KJV, fairly typical, has the following, which seems to provide a clear antecedent for the pronouns *them* and *they* (italics added):

> 4 Deliver the poor and needy: rid *them* out of the hand of the
> wicked.
>
> 5 *They* know not, neither will *they* understand; *they* walk on in
> darkness:
>
> all the foundations of the earth are out of course.

The possibility does exist, however, that God speaks v. 5 in a theatrical aside about the failed "gods" to someone else—the narrator, perhaps—in order to give a sardonic edge to his speech, but the KJV and most other versions do not clarify or privilege that understanding.

The NRSV, much less typical, supplies quotation marks, but they complicate matters further:

> 4 Rescue the weak and the needy;
>
> deliver them from the hand of the wicked."
>
> [*God is speaking; the quotation closes after "wicked."*]
>
> 5 They have neither knowledge nor understanding,
>
> [*The poem's narrator resumes speaking.*]
>
> they walk around in darkness;
>
> all the foundations of the earth are shaken.
>
> 6 I say, "You are gods,
>
> [*The narrator continues speaking and quotes himself.*]
>
> children of the Most High, all of you [. . .]."

Obviously, the NRSV has a more active narrator/persona and a less-quoted God; however, the pronoun-reference ambiguity remains. It has simply been moved into the mouth of another speaker, the narrator.

A third possibility that the Hebrew apparently allows, though, is particularly attractive for reading Herbert's "Humilitie" against the backdrop of Psalm 82. Not alone in the history of biblical translation and paraphrase, the Sidney Psalter of 1599 assumes that in Ps 82:4–5 God is still addressing the "gods" directly and that *they* are the ones who walk in darkness:

> [4] 'This you should do. But what do ye?
> You nothing know, you nothing see:
> [5] No light, no law; fie, fie, the very ground
> Becomes unsound,
> So right, wrong, all, your faults confound.

In those lines, Mary Sidney Herbert, Countess of Pembroke, unambiguously uses the second-person pronouns to identify God's primary audience, the "gods," as the benighted ones.[49] The Oxford New English Bible (1961, 1970) makes a similar move:

> 4 You ought to rescue the weak and the poor,
> and save them from the clutches of wicked men.
> 5 But you know nothing, you understand nothing,
> You walk in the dark
> While earth's foundations are giving way.

The Sidney and NEB renderings simplify the situation: verse 5 is just a descriptive piece of God's direct indictment of the "gods," who are benighted know-nothings without salutary effect in the crumbling world.

Wilcox notes that "[t]he most important literary influence on Herbert's poetic forms was undoubtedly the translation of *Psalms* by Mary Sidney and her brother Philip."[50] Given that influence, it is quite possible that Herbert's understanding of Psalm 82, which is clearly a piece of theatre anyway, centered upon the theatrically effective verbal broadside uttered by God against the malfeasant "gods." Mary Sidney's language is exceptionally strong, full of pounding

49. Sidney and Sidney, *The Sidney Psalter*, 161.
50. Wilcox, *The English Poems*, xxviii.

alliteration ("light"/"law," "fie"/"fie," "right"/"wrong"), various dark and shrill assonances ("No"/"no," "fie"/"fie"), and that growling triple rhyme. When Herbert's Crow brings the Peacock's plume and chaos erupts among the Virtues, we seem to have a refracted and extended image of vice-regent irresponsibility, culpability, and stumbling ineffectiveness. The tears of Humility are a theatrical flourish akin to God's palpable disappointment in 82:6–7, as if Humility were saying, "I thought you were gods! But what wrangling wretches you have turned out to be!"

In the allegorical world of Herbert's "Humilitie," the "beasts and fowls" are in the position of the afflicted in relation to the Virtues. This I consider a Herbertian refraction of the psalm that counsels administrative temperance and compassion. Whether or not the beasts and fowls have been abroad causing trouble in the realm, they receive harsh treatment by the Virtues, who sit "hand in hand" to be given "tokens of submission." As the poem develops, the *topos* of "judging unjustly" is clearly in evidence; the sub-*topos* of "accept[ing] the persons of the wicked" also shows up in the Virtues' trying to accept the probably purloined plume from the Crow, who is represented as the most current malefactor. As I have explained earlier, the very notion of temperance requires a "frugality" of governance, of resource-use, that can recognize what is necessary and proper as well as what is unnecessary and improper. In both psychological and social terms, some expression of the passions is necessary; some is not. Whether we read "Humilitie" as a psychomachia or as a sociopolitical narrative, it is an exemplum of prodigally intemperate governance,[51] exactly what Psalm 82 condemns in general terms.

I am not suggesting that a rigorous one-to-one relationship exists between Psalm 82 and "Humilitie" but that (a) similar administrative malfeasance in the *polis* is generally named in the former and specifically narrated in the latter and that (b) the frames of both poems (particularly the openings) bear striking resemblances. Since

---

51. The intemperate actions of the corrupt Virtues in Herbert's poem are not analogous to God's judgment and sentencing of the lesser "gods" in Psalm 82. They are analogous to the "unjust" judgments of the "gods" to which 82:2 refers. My basic claim about "Humilitie" is that Herbert seems to have filled in the Ps 82 gaps imaginatively by presenting a particular narrative with specific story-stuff.

Herbert consciously and, probably, unconsciously referred to the Psalms hundreds of times in *The Temple*, and since his collection called "The Church" bears many resemblances to the Hebrew Psalter, it seems sensible to consider what devices, *topoi*, and attitudes of so dramatic a poem as Psalm 82 might appear, refracted, in some single poem in Herbert's collection. Gottlieb clearly senses the unusual quality of "Humilitie," which he considers "a parable of the complicity between the psychological dynamics and social institutions of control and disorder" and thus "a poem worthy of Blake—and Foucault."[52] I think it stands in Herbert's collection much as Psalm 82 does in the Psalter.

Like Psalm 82 in its collection, "Humilitie" momentarily brings Herbert's refracted psalter to a high pitch of social concern in its own. Most of the other arguably social-concern passages in "The Church" are brief, and most are heavily subordinated to discussion of spiritual concerns. "The Quidditie," for example, one of the five poems in the "contempt of court" sequence that includes "Humilitie," refers at length to poetry's lack of social empowerment but brushes the issue off the table by concluding that its spiritual empowerment in the persona's society with God is much the better. "Repentance" briefly brings up the basis for social compassion in its second stanza but does not pursue the topic, moving on into spiritual confession and petition:

> [W]e are all
> To sorrows old,
> If Life be told
> From what life feeleth, Adams fall.
> O let thy height of mercie then
> Compassionate short-breathed men.

Personal spiritual disorientation is by far the dominant sort in "The Church," but social disorientation makes some appearances, sometimes to provide an analog for a spiritual problem—as in "Unkindnesse," wherein, as I have said, references to the proper management of human friendship become the ironic antithesis of the persona's treatment of Christ:

---

52. Gottlieb, "From 'Content' to 'Affliction' (III)," 483.

> If any touch my friend, or his good name;
> It is my honour and my love to free
> His blasted fame
> From the least spot or thought of blame.
> I could not use a friend, as I use Thee.

The primary issue here is of the First Great Commandment type ("Thou shalt Love the Lord thy God with all thy heart"); the expository support is of the Second Great Commandment type ("Thou shalt love [. . .] thy neighbor as thyself").[53] Against such a backdrop of mostly pietistic poems, "Humilitie" seems like a rare prismatic flower of social concern.

---

53. Luke 10:27 (KJV).

Appendix

Poems from "The Church" Collection Having Significant Social-Concern Aspects

WILCOX'S COLLECTION OF ALL extant Herbert poems includes fifteen "Miscellaneous" poems not included in The Temple and three poems that open The Temple: "The Dedication," "The Church-porch," and "Superliminare." There are 163 poems in the section called "The Church"; twenty-five at least partly address or refer to issues of social concern (SC), a category that largely overlaps with Bellinger's Community Lament; thus, 15.34 percent of "The Church" arguably brings up SC topics. In Bellinger's analysis of the Psalms, he finds seventeen of 150 (11.33 percent) to be of "Community Lament" sort.

Wilcox No.	Title	SC Line(s)	SC Heavily Subordinated to Spiritual Argument	SC Moderately Prominent and Autonomous	SC Very Strong and Salient
26	Redemption	9–14	✓		
33	Sinne (I)	2–4	✓		
34	Affliction (I)	37–42, 57–60	✓		
44	Jordan (I)	whole poem, but esp. 11–15		✓	
46	The H. Scriptures (I)	13–14	✓		
55	Church-monuments	whole poem	✓		
60	Trinitie Sunday	1, 3, 7–8		✓	
61	Content	whole poem, but esp. 13–16, 21–32			✓
62	The Quidditie	1–12		✓	
63	Humilitie	whole poem			✓
65	Constancie	whole poem			✓
69	Avarice	whole poem			✓
72	Employment (II)	1–5, 11–17, 21–30		✓	
80	Lent	7–12, 22–24, 28–30, 46–48	✓		
84	Man	13–17	✓		
86	Unkindnesse	whole poem	✓		
90	Charms and Knots	3–6, 9–14			✓
117	Giddinesse	3–4, 9–12, 21–24		✓	
124	Divinitie	13–20	✓		
129	Church-rents and schismes	whole poem			✓
136	An Offering	9–12	✓		
148	The Priesthood	19–42		✓	
156	The Answer	whole poem			✓
166	The Foil	whole poem, but esp. 7–8		✓	
170	The Invitation	31–36	✓		

Bibliography

Alter, Robert, trans. *The Book of Psalms: A Translation with Commentary.* New York: Norton, 2007.

Bellinger, W. H. *Psalms: Reading and Studying the Book of Praises.* Peabody, MA: Hendrickson, 1990.

Bloch, Chana. *Spelling the Word: George Herbert and the Bible.* Berkeley: University of California Press, 1985.

Brennan, Michael G. "Licensing the Sidney Psalms for the Press in the 1640s." *Notes & Queries* 31/3 (1984) 304.

Brueggemann, Walter. *The Message of the Psalms: A Theological Commentary.* Minneapolis: Augsburg, 1984.

Cicero, Marcus Tullius. *Cicero's Tusculan Disputations.* Translated by C. D. Yonge. New York: Harper, 1877.

———. *Tusculan Disputations.* Translated by J. E. King. Loeb Classical Library 141. Cambridge, MA: Harvard University Press, 1927.

Fairclough, Norman. *Discourse and Social Change.* Cambridge: Polity, 1992.

Fish, Stanley. *The Living Temple: George Herbert and Catechizing.* Berkeley: University of California Press, 1978.

Freer, Coburn. *Music for a King: George Herbert's Style and the Metrical Psalms.* Baltimore: Johns Hopkins University Press, 1972.

Gottlieb, Sidney. "From 'Content' to 'Affliction' (III): Herbert's Anti-Court Sequence." *English Literary Renaissance* 23/3 (1993) 472–89.

———. "Herbert's Political Allegory of 'Humilitie.'" *Huntington Library Quarterly* 52 (1989) 469–80.

Gottwald, Norman K. *The Hebrew Bible: A Socio-Literary Introduction.* Philadelphia: Fortress, 1985.

Gunkel, Hermann. *Introduction to Psalms: The Genres of the Religious Lyric of Israel.* Edited by Joachim Begrich. Translated by James D. Nogalski. Macon, GA: Mercer University Press, 1998.

———. *The Psalms: Form-Critical Introduction.* Philadephia: Fortress, 1967.

Herbert, George. *The English Poems of George Herbert.* Edited by Helen Wilcox. Cambridge: Cambridge University Press, 2007.

Hodgkins, Christopher. *Authority, Church, and Society in George Herbert: Return to the Middle Way.* Columbia: University of Missouri Press, 1993.

Lewis, Paul W., and Martin William Mittelstadt, eds. *What's So Liberal about the Liberal Arts? Integrated Approaches to Christian Formation.* Eugene, OR: Pickwick, 2016.

Lewis-Anthony, Justin. *If You Meet George Herbert on the Road, Kill Him: Radically Re-thinking Priestly Ministry.* London: Mowbray, 2009.

Lull, Janis. *The Poem in Time: Reading George Herbert's Revisions of "The Church."* Newark: University of Delaware Press, 1990.

Mulder, John R. "*The Temple* as Picture." In *"Too Rich to Clothe the Sunne": Essays on George Herbert,* edited by Claude J. Summers and Ted-Larry Pebworth, 3–14. Pittsburgh: University of Pittsburgh Press, 1980.

Patrides, C. A. *Figures in a Renaissance Context.* Edited by Claude J. Summers and Ted-Larry Pebworth. Ann Arbor: University of Michigan Press, 1989.

Quitslund, Beth. "Teaching Us How to Sing? The Peculiarity of the Sidney Psalter." *Sidney Journal* 23/1–2 (2005) 109–10.

Ray, Robert H. "Herbert's Seventeenth-Century Reputation: A Summary and New Considerations." *George Herbert Journal* 9/2 (1986) 1–15.

Rollin, Roger B. "Self-Created Artifact: The Speaker and the Reader in The Temple." In *"Too Rich to Clothe the Sunne": Essays on George Herbert,* edited by Claude J. Summers and Ted-Larry Pebworth, 147–61. Pittsburgh: University of Pittsburgh Press, 1980.

Sidney, Philip, and Mary Sidney. *The Sidney Psalter: The Psalms of Sir Philip and Mary Sidney.* Edited by Hannibal Hamlin et al. Oxford: Oxford University Press, 2009.

Singleton, Marion White. *God's Courtier: Configuring a Different Grace in George Herbert's Temple.* Cambridge: Cambridge University Press, 1987.

Strier, Richard. "Ironic Humanism in *The Temple.*" In *"Too Rich to Clothe the Sunne": Essays on George Herbert,* edited by Claude J. Summers and Ted-Larry Pebworth, 33–52. Pittsburgh: University of Pittsburgh Press, 1980.

Summers, Joseph. *George Herbert: His Religion and Art.* Binghamton: Center for Medieval and Early Renaissance Studies, 1981.

Summers, Joseph, and Ted-Larry Pebworth, eds. *"Too Rich to Clothe the Sunne": Essays on George Herbert.* Pittsburgh: University of Pittsburgh Press, 1980.

Trotter, James M. "Death of the אלהים in Psalm 82." *Journal of Biblical Literature* 131/2 (2012) 221–39.

Wall, John N. *Transformations of the Word: Spenser, Herbert, Vaughan.* Athens: University of Georgia Press, 1988.

Westermann, Claus. *Praise and Lament in the Psalms.* Atlanta: John Knox, 1981.

Wilcox, Helen, ed. *The English Poems of George Herbert.* Cambridge: Cambridge University Press, 2007.

Wohlers, Charles, ed. *The Book of Common Prayer—1559.* http://justus.anglican.org/resources/bcp/1559/BCP_1559.htm.